It's All a Matter of
Attitude!

Stories that inspire faith and courage

Published by:
Gita Publishing House
Sadhu Vaswani Mission,
10, Sadhu Vaswani Path,
Pune 411 001, (India).
gph@sadhuvaswani.org
www.dadavaswanisbooks.org

Third Edition

ISBN: 978-93-80743-28-8

Cover Design: Lavesh Milani

Printed by:
Mehta Offset Pvt. Ltd.
Mehta House,
A-16, Naraina Industrial Area II,
New Delhi 110 028, (India).
Phone : +91-11-45670222
info@mehtaoffset.com

It's All A Matter Of
Attitude!
Stories that inspire
faith and courage

J.P. Vaswani

Compiled by
Dr. Prabha Sampath
and
Krishna Kumari

Gita Publishing House
Pune, (India).
www.dadavaswanisbooks.org

Other Books By Dada J.P. Vaswani

English:
10 Commandments of A Successful Marriage
108 Pearls of Practical Wisdom
108 Simple Prayers of A Simple Man
108 Thoughts on Success
114 Thoughts on Love
A Little Book of Life
A Treasure of Quotes
Around The Camp Fire
Begin The Day With God
Burn Anger Before Anger Burns You
Daily Inspiration
Daily Inspiration (Booklet)
Destination Happiness
Dewdrops of Love
Does God Have Favourites?
Formula For Prosperity
Gateways to Heaven
God In Quest of Man
Good Parenting
What You Would Like To know About Hinduism
I am a Sindhi
In 2012 All Will Be Well
Joy Peace Pills
Kill Fear Before Fear Kills You
Ladder of Abhyasa
Lessons Life Has Taught Me
Life After Death
Management Moment by Moment
Mantras For Peace Of Mind
Many Paths: One Goal
Nearer, My God, To Thee!
New Education Can Make the World New
Peace or Perish
Positive Power of Thanksgiving
Questions Answered
Sadhu Vaswani : His Life And Teachings
Saints For You and Me
Saints With A Difference
Secrets of Health And Happiness
Short Sketches of Saints Known & Unknown
Sketches of Saints Known & Unknown
Stop Complaining: Start Thanking!
Swallow Irritation Before Irritation Swallows You
Teachers are Sculptors
The Little Book of Freedom From Stress
The Little Book of Prayer
The Little Book of Service
The Little Book of Success
The Little Book of Wisdom
The Little Book of Yoga
The Magic of Forgiveness
The Perfect Relationship: Guru and Disciple
The Seven Commandments of the Bhagavad Gita
The Terror Within
The Way of Abhyasa (How To Meditate)
Thus Have I Been Taught
Tips For Teenagers
What You Would Like To know About Karma
Why Do Good People Suffer?
You Are Not Alone God Is With You!

Story Books:
101 Stories For You And Me

25 Stories For Children and also for Teens
Break The Habit
More Snacks For The Soul
Snacks For The Soul
The Lord Provides
The Heart of a Mother
The King of Kings
The One Thing Needful
The Patience of Purna
The Power of Good Deeds
The Power of Thought
Trust Me All in All or Not at All
Whom Do You Love the Most
You Can Make A Difference

In Hindi:
Aalwar Santon Ki Mahan Gaathaayen
Atmik Jalpaan
Atmik Poshan
Bhakton Ki Uljhanon Kaa Saral Upaai
Bhale Logon Ke Saath Bura Kyon?
Brindavan Ka Balak
Dainik Prerna
Dar Se Mukti Paayen
Ishwar Tujhe Pranam
Jiski Jholi Mein Hain Pyaar
Krodh Ko Jalayen Swayam Ko Nahin
Laghu Kathayein
Mrutyu Hai Dwar... Phir Kya?
Nava Pushp (Bhajans In Hindi and Sindhi)
Prarthna ki Shakti
Pyar Ka Masiha
Sadhu Vaswani: Unkaa Jeevan Aur Shikshaayen
Safal Vivah Ke Dus Rahasya
Santon Ki Leela

In Marathi:
Krodhala Shaanth Kara, Krodhane Ghala Ghalnya Purvee (Burn Anger Before Anger Burns You)
Jiski Jholi Mein Hain Pyaar
Life After Death
Pilgrim of Love
Sind and the Sindhis
Sufi Sant (Sufi Saints of East and West)
What You Would Like To Know About Karma

In Kannada:
101 Stories For You And Me
Burn Anger Before Anger Burns You
Life After Death
Tips for Teenagers
Why do Good People Suffer

In Telugu:
Burn Anger Before Anger Burns You
Life after Death
What You Would Like To Know About Karma

In Spanish:
Aprenda A Controlar Su Ira (Burn Anger Before Anger burns You)
Bocaditos Para el Alma (Snacks for the Soul)
Dios (Daily Meeting With God)
El Bein Quentu Hagas, Regresa (The Good You Do Returns)
Encontro Diario Com Deus (Daily Appontment With God)
Inicia Tu Dia Con Dios (Begin The Day With God)
L'Inspiration Quotidienne (Daily Inspiration)

Mas Bocaditos Para el Alma (More Snacks for the Soul)
Mata al miedo antes de que el miedo te mate (Kill Fear Before Fear Kills you)
Queme La Ira Antes Que La Ira Lo Queme A Usted(Burn Anger Before Anger Burns You)
Sita Diario ku Dios (I Luv U, God!)
Todo es Cuestion de Actitud! (Its All A Matter of Attitude)
Vida despu'es de la Muerte (Life After Death)

In Arabic:
Daily Appointment With God
Daily Inspiration

In Chinese:
Daily Appointment With God

In Dutch:
Begin The Day With God

In Bahasa:
A Little Book of Success
A Little Book of Wisdom
Burn Anger Before Anger burns You
Life After Death

In Gujrati:
Its All A Matter of Attitude

In Oriya:
Burn Anger Before Anger burns You
More Snacks For the Soul
Pilgrim of Love
Snacks For The Soul
Why Do Good People Suffer

In Russian:
What would you like to Know about Karma

In Sindhi:
Burn Anger Before Anger Burns You
Jaade Pireen Kaare Pandh
Munhjee Dil Te Lagee Laahootiyun Saan
Why Do Good People Suffer
Vatan Je Vannan De

In Tamil:
10 Commandments of a Successful Marriage
Burn Anger Before Anger burns You
Daily Appointment with God
Its All a Matter of Attitude
Kill Fear Before Fear Kills You
More Snacks For the Soul
Secrets of Health and Happiness
Snacks For The Soul
Why Do Good People Suffer

In Latvian:
The Magic of Forgiveness

Other Publications:
Recipe Books:
90 Vegetarian Sindhi Recipes
Di-li-cious Vegetarian Recipes
Simply Vegetarian

Books on Dada J. P. Vaswani:
A Pilgrim of Love
Dada J.P. Vaswani: His Life and Teachings
Dada J.P. Vaswani's Historic Visit to Sind
Dost Thou Keep Memory
How To Embrace Pain
Living Legend
Moments with a Master

Contents

1. It's All a Matter of Attitude — 9
2. Looking On The Bright Side — 11
3. Don't Anticipate Trouble — 13
4. My Heart Got There First! — 16
5. No Names Please! — 18
6. No Reply! — 20
7. The Spirit of Hospitality — 22
8. Believe and Achieve! — 25
9. We Can Create Our Future Destiny — 27
10. We Are What We Think — 28
11. Service with a Smile — 30
12. I'm One of You — 31
13. The Snails of Sin — 33
14. An Effective Prescription — 36
15. You Fed Me When I Was Hungry — 38
16. Not Suitable — 40
17. A Photo Opportunity — 42
18. God Is Watching You! — 43
19. Determination Conquers All — 45

20.	No Job Is Menial	46
21.	Not for Me!	48
22.	Giving without Questions	49
23.	It's All in the Mind	52
24.	Look Within for Your Treasure!	55
25.	A Change of Attire	58
26.	I Ask for Nothing More!	60
27.	The Secret of Charlie's Success	62
28.	Help Your Brother!	64
29.	His Stores Are Never Empty!	66
30.	Compassion in Action	68
31.	Let My Music Move Them!	70
32.	Life Is a Loan	72
33.	He Answered My Prayer!	74
34.	Bad Luck, Good Luck	76
35.	Helping a Friend	79
36.	Rivals and Friends	81
37.	Fix Your Goal	82
38.	Life, Not Words	83
39.	The Prayer of Surrender	85
40.	It's Krishna!	88
41.	What's Inside Counts!	90
42.	He Is There When You Need Him	92
43.	A Beggar Becomes a Businessman	95
44.	The Best News	97

45.	Service – A *Sadhana*	99
46.	Never, Never, Never Give Up!	101
47.	The Fire-Worshipper	103
48.	I Have a Room for You!	106
49.	The Widow's Mite	107
50.	Charity with Courtesy	109
51.	Not for Fame or Money	111
52.	Here's Something Better!	113
53.	The Prayer of Affirmation	116
54.	And Sri Krishna Came …	118
55.	The Lord's Way	122
56.	A Gift to God	123
57.	A Humble Request	124
58.	Slow and Steady	125
59.	Get Connected to God!	127
60.	The Tenfold Gift	129
61.	Gandhi and Tagore	133
62.	Book of Noble Conduct	135
63.	One Thing at a Time	137
64.	Forgiveness, the Best Lubricant	139
65.	Let Us Thank the Lord	141
66.	Painting Feet on a Snake	143
67.	Just Laugh It Off!	145
68.	Abu Othman and His Host	147
69.	Write it on Sand!	149

70.	O, Let Them Live!	152
71.	The Secret of Yoga	154
72.	Finding God	156
73.	My *All* for the Guru	157
74.	The Devoted Servant	159
75.	No Room for Fear	161

It's All a Matter of Attitude

Dr. S. Radhakrishnan, the great philosopher and former President of India, made his first visit to the United States when John F. Kennedy was the President. The weather was dark and stormy in Washington; and when Dr. Radhakrishnan alighted from the plane, it began to rain cats and dogs, as the expression goes.

The young American President greeted his Indian counterpart with a warm handshake and a smile. "I'm so sorry we have such bad weather during your visit," he remarked courteously.

The philosopher-statesman smiled. "We can't change bad things, Mr. President," he observed. "But we can change our attitude towards them."

A few years ago I was in Delhi, when I was invited by Doordarshan to visit their studios. There I met a wonderful man. He had lost both his arms in an accident. But he had a positive attitude. He trained his feet so that he could take up the job of composing in a press. With a smile on his face and a feeling of joy, he said, "I earn Rs 500 a month. I am not a burden on anyone."

There was another man whom I met in Pune. He was sitting by the wayside, and he was crippled beneath the waist. He only had stumps instead of legs.

"What happened to you?" I asked him.

"Nothing!" he replied. "I was born this way."

"May I ask, who takes care of you, my friend?" I enquired.

"My mother, and above all, God."

"Do you find it difficult, or inconvenient to move about?"

"Do you find it difficult, or inconvenient that you don't have wings?" he asked me. "Don't you think it would be far better if you could fly on your own, rather than wait to catch a plane?"

"Life is a matter of habit," he added. "If you start complaining, there is so much to complain about. It is the attitude that counts."

10

Looking on the Bright Side

A world famous shoe manufacturer took a decision to expand his business, by setting up a new branch in a remote, little-known country. He called up one of his marketing managers and asked him to take the next flight to the country and explore the possibility of setting up a new factory there.

The young executive flew out the very next day. But within 24 hours of reaching there he called up his boss. "This place is no good for our business," he said gloomily. "People do not wear shoes out here. We had better forget any notion of setting up a factory here. It simply won't do. And I am catching the next flight home."

The boss was highly dissatisfied with the report. He had set his heart on doing what he wanted. So he called up another young manager and sent him out with the same order.

Within a few hours of landing there, the young man called up in great excitement. "This place is unbelievable," he exclaimed. "Our business is going to boom out here. These people don't even know what shoes are like. When we introduce shoes here, we shall have a whole, new, untapped market. Send in our planners and designers as soon as you can. We must set up a factory here and we shall win all the way!"

What a difference a positive attitude can make!

Don't Anticipate Trouble

There was a woman whose daughter was late in returning home one night. The mother imagined that all sorts of misfortunes had befallen the child. By about 9 o'clock, she began calling up the city hospitals to find out if a girl had been admitted that evening. She was about to ring the police station to file a complaint, when the girl walked into the house, happily, humming a tune. The mother was, by this time, reduced to the state of a nervous wreck.

"Wh-where were you all this while?" she said to her daughter, sobbing. "Do you know what I've gone through in the last two hours?"

"Oh, mamma, why do you fuss so much?" laughed the girl. "I met my school friend Leela, and we got talking about the good old days. The time just flew past and we both hardly noticed it. But here I am, and I'm hungry! What's for dinner tonight?"

13

It was Jesus who said: "Sufficient unto the day is the evil thereof." We have all been endowed with sufficient strength. God has blessed us with the means and resources to tackle our life each day. God does not dwell in the Heavens above, He is here in the heart within you. He gives you the strength to face the troubles that you may have to face on any given day.

Anticipating troubles leads to unnecessary worry. We are told that worry is derived from two different Anglo Saxon roots which mean, "harm" and "wolf". True, worry is harmful and it bites and tears us even as a wolf mauls a lamb. A little worry or anxiety can be helpful, for it keeps us on the alert, and prepares us for action. But excessive worry has the opposite effect – it paralyses the will and makes us unfit for action. It clouds our vision and distracts the thinking process.

An old story tells us of an angel who met a man carrying a heavy sack on his back.

"What is it that you carry on your back, my friend?" enquired the angel.

"My worries," sighed the man. "Truly, they are a terrible burden."

14

"Put down the sack," said the angel, "and let me see your worries."

When the sack was opened, it was empty! The man was astonished. He had two great worries: one was about yesterday, which he now saw was past; the other of tomorrow, which had not yet arrived!

The angel told him, "You have no worries. Throw the sack away."

And so it is that we have the wise saying, "In trouble to be troubled is to have your troubles doubled."

My Heart Got There First!

On a cold winter's day, with the temperature below zero, an old pilgrim was making his way to a shrine in the Himalayas.

"My man," exclaimed a fellow traveller who passed by, "how will you ever get there in such cold weather?"

"My heart got there first," replied the man cheerfully. "It's easy for the rest of me to follow!"

Within each and every one of us is a tremendous potential to overcome obstacles and achieve success; to face difficulties and overcome them. There is just one thing we have to do to tap this vast potential, this tremendous power: we must believe in ourselves.

No Names Please!

There is something called the National Bone Marrow Donor Programme which is being run in the United States. Bone marrow transplant can help to save the life of a patient suffering from leukaemia and related disorders. Donors who wish to join this programme have to register their names with the local hospital authorities and undergo a blood test. Whenever a patient needs a bone marrow transplant, the Association contacts the donors. They undergo a series of tests to confirm the match. Finally, the donor is requested to go to the hospital where the transplant surgery is to take place. The process of donating bone marrow is not very complicated. Donors describe it as being "just a little painful." They are often discharged on the evening of the same day.

The donor and recipient are always kept anonymous. The donor never gets to know whose life he has saved – and the patient does not get to know whom he must thank for helping to save his life.

What a beautiful lesson this is for us all, on silent service!

No Reply!

One day, an old man came to meet me. He was in a bitter, angry frame of mind. "How is this?" he complained. "I have written no less than five letters to you and you have not answered even one of them!"

I was surprised, for I always try to reply to every one of my letters promptly. And I did not remember having received even one of his letters. I told him so.

"I have written five letters to you, not one or two or three," he insisted.

In fact, he *had* written five letters. His daughter, who accompanied him, explained the mystery. "Father," she said, "it is true you have written five letters, but they are all lying in your drawer. You have not posted any one of them."

Our prayers are like these letters that are never posted. They lack the power of suction; they do not move forward. Therefore, they are not answered. The letters that are posted, reach the addressee. The prayers that come out of the very depth of our being, are invariably always answered. There is yet another reason why our prayers are not answered – some of them are so ridiculous, so absurd, that God in His Divine Wisdom, ignores them.

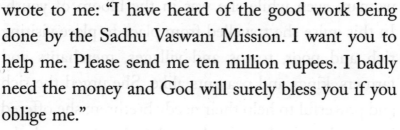

Some years ago, I received a letter from a perfect stranger. He wrote to me: "I have heard of the good work being done by the Sadhu Vaswani Mission. I want you to help me. Please send me ten million rupees. I badly need the money and God will surely bless you if you oblige me."

The whole thing was so preposterous that no one would take such a letter seriously!

The Spirit of Hospitality

Avvaiyar was a well-known and much beloved woman saint in ancient Tamil Nadu. It is said of her that she renounced worldly life and assumed the form and shape of an old, grey-haired woman, even while she was in the bloom of youth. In this guise she travelled from place to place visiting rich and poor, towns and villages, merchants and farmers, kings and peasants alike. She urged the rich and powerful to help their needy brethren; she offered her good counsel to people so that they may seek the truth and devote their lives to the cause of goodness. She was loved and respected wherever she went; she was a welcome guest at the palaces of princes, as in the humble cottages of the landless labourers.

Avvaiyar returned their kindness and affection by writing of her encounters with them in her immortal verses. For she was also a gifted poet, whose works are still studied and recited with love and reverence by Tamil speaking people everywhere.

On a dark and rainy night, Avvaiyar was forced to knock at the door of a cottage in the woods, seeking shelter from the stormy weather.

The door of the cottage was opened by Aivel, the chieftain of the local tribe. Aivel was indeed a chieftain, but he was not rich in the wealth of the world. He and his tribe owned a small tract of land and a few heads of cattle, which they farmed and shared as a collective.

On this stormy night, Aivel was thrilled to see Avvaiyar at his doorstep. He welcomed her into his humble cottage and offered her a blanket to stop her from shivering. He saw that the ageing saint was famished. He bustled about the cottage, getting a meal ready for her. In a short while he laid before her, a bowl of goat's milk and a few wild tubers from the woods, which he had cooked with great care.

"Dear mother," he said to her in deep humility, "you have been entertained by royalty, and feasted by princes and powerful men. Tonight, this is the best fare that I am able to offer to you. Please accept this food and bless me."

Avvaiyar was deeply moved by the kindness and hospitality of this humble man. The food and the shelter he offered to her were indeed nobler than the banquets and feasts of kings. She blessed Aivel and immortalised him in verses which are known today under the name "The compassion of Aivel".

Our ancient scripture equates guests with God: *Atithi devo bhava.* Scholars of Sanskrit have commented on the significance of the term *atithi* – *a+tithi,* or one who arrives without prior notice of day or date; in other words, an unexpected guest. Even such visitors to our homes should be treated with love and respect. We may not be in a position to prepare an elaborate meal for them; but we should invite them to share our homely meals with courtesy and warmth. This indeed is the true spirit of hospitality.

Believe and Achieve!

Walter Davis was a great athlete and he achieved everything he believed in. As a boy, he contracted infantile paralysis, and the doctors feared that he might not be able to walk again.

His mother's loving care and attention put the boy back on his feet. As he began to walk slowly, he saw a boy doing the high jump and thought to himself: "That is something I would love to do!" So he began practising the high jump, until he became very good at it.

But his legs were still weak, and serious competition was out of the question for him. He kept up his painstaking efforts to strengthen them. When he married, his wife understood his aspirations and said to him, "Walter, it is not enough to have power in your legs. You must have power in your mind!"

She coined a new phrase for him: The strength of belief. This, she said would bring greater strength to his legs.

Strength of belief took Walter Davis to great heights. Eventually, it helped him create a world record. He cleared the bar at six feet eleven and five-eighths inches – propelled by his strength of belief. The boy they said might never walk again became the High Jump Champion of the world! Belief was his strength – and so he believed and achieved!

We Can Create Our Future Destiny

There was a lady who belonged to the respected Lin family of ancient China. The Lins were pious, compassionate and generous. Every day the lady would make rice balls to distribute among the poor.

As many pieces as people asked for, she would give them.

There was a Tao monk who asked for six or seven rice balls every day. He continued to come to her house for three years. She gave him whatever he asked for, without once expressing displeasure. Such was her sincerity and kindness that the Tao monk said to her, that future generations of the family would benefit from her generosity. "The number of your descendants who will prosper in life will be equivalent to the number of seeds in a pound of sesame seeds," he said, as he blessed her for her compassion and generosity. True enough, her descendants flourished and grew prosperous.

We Are What We Think

Two American soldiers had been prisoners of war in Japan during the Second World War. Eventually they both survived, and went on to lead their lives back home. They met at a reunion 50 years later, in 1995. By now, Japan and US were actually allies. Everything had changed.

One asked the other, "Have you forgiven those who imprisoned you?"

"No, I haven't," replied the second man vehemently. "Never, never shall I forgive them."

"In that case," said the first man softly, "somehow you are still in their prison."

The Buddha's teachings in the great *Dhammapada* begins with these memorable lines:

We are what we think.
All that we are arises with our thoughts.
With our thoughts we make the world.
Speak or act with an impure mind
And trouble will follow you
As the wheel follows the ox that draws the cart.
We are what we think.
All that we are arises with our thoughts.
With our thoughts we make the world.
Speak or act with a pure mind
And happiness will follow you
As your shadow, unshakable.

Service with a Smile

There was a millionaire who had given away the larger portion of her vast fortune to a Mission, which provided humanitarian services to poor people. She herself was old and handicapped, but she would regularly attend the evening meetings at the Mission, standing at the door to greet everyone who entered or left the *satsang* hall.

One day, a distinguished visitor was being taken round the Mission. Seeing the old lady at the door, he asked her, "What is your part in the wonderful work that is going on here?"

The old lady did not boast of her donations to the cause. She only said, "I smile the people in, and I smile them out!"

"That is wonderful!" exclaimed the visitor. "That is the most valuable service one can offer in the world where so many are downcast and discouraged!"

I'm One of You!

There was an English woman who travelled to South Africa to serve the black people in that country. On her first day in the country, she took a basketful of gifts for children – toys, dolls, games, dresses, sweets and so on. She was eager to give it all away to the poor black children, but she was dismayed to find that the children would not come near her – even though they looked at the gifts with great longing. When she approached the children to offer the gifts to them, they retreated hastily.

She thought about it for a while and came to the conclusion that it was the colour of her skin which was the problem. The children were scared of her because she was white and they were black.

She hit upon a novel idea. The next day, she put on a dark shade of make-up, so that she looked like a coloured woman. She carried the basket of gifts into the same slums – and now, the children ran to her, crying, "Auntie, give me the doll!" "Lady, can I have the ball?" "Can you give me some chocolate?" and so on. Her joy knew no bounds.

It is very important that we must have this sense of identification with the people whom we seek to serve.

The Snails of Sin

beautiful swan flew down and alighted on the banks of a stream. She saw a crane wading in the shallow waters, near the muddy bank, looking for snails.

The crane cast a glance at the swan and asked, "Where have you come from? I haven't seen you in these parts earlier!"

"I come from heaven," replied the swan.

"And where is *that*, if one may ask?" enquired the crane, his eyes not leaving the mud in which he was looking for snails.

"Have you never heard of heaven, up above this earth, where there is perfect peace and joy?" the swan asked in surprise.

"No, never," replied the crane. "I lead a full and busy life here. The stream gets muddier every year and there is no dearth of snails. Where do I have time to think of foreign lands?"

In beautiful, eloquent terms, the swan described the heaven world – its pearly gates, its streets of gold, its river of life as clear as crystal.

"Are there any snails in the river?" the crane interrupted.

"No, of course not," said the swan.

"Then you can keep heaven to yourself," said the crane, moving away as it searched along the slimy bank for more food, "I can't do without snails!"

Many of us, alas, are like the crane. We are obsessed with the slimy snails – the passing pleasures of this world – and ignore heaven and its rewards. Unless we set our sights on higher things, we cannot attain to heaven.

An Effective Prescription

liver Goldsmith, the English writer, had qualified himself to be a doctor – though he did not practise medicine as a career. One day, an old woman who had heard how kind-hearted the poet was, came to see him. She said to him with tears in her eyes, "Sir, my husband is very ill. None of the doctors will come to see him because we do not have money to pay them. I beg you to come and see him."

Goldsmith accompanied her to her home, which was cold, bare and bereft of all comfort. The woman's husband lay on a bed; he was weak and emaciated. There was no fire in the hearth. Goldsmith's caring gaze took in everything at a glance.

After a few words with the couple, Goldsmith took leave of them. He said to the woman, "I shall send some pills to you, Madame. Please give them to the patient according to my prescription."

He went home quickly and put ten guineas into a pill-box. He labelled the box with the prescription: *One to be used every day to buy food, milk and coal. Be patient and hopeful.*

A messenger was despatched to hand the box over to the woman. Needless to say, the 'prescription' worked a miracle on the old couple, who had been suffering due to poverty and neglect. It was not long before they came to visit their kind 'doctor' and thanked him for his timely help.

You Fed Me When I Was Hungry

There is a beautiful story by Tolstoy entitled, "He Who Sees His Neighbour Has Seen God." It tells us of an old and devout shoemaker, who dreams that Jesus Christ is going to visit him the next day. He sits at the window of his basement dwelling and watches passers-by, eagerly looking for Christ. He sees a desperate woman with a crying child – he invites her to come in, comforts her, offers her food and helps her as much as he can.

Next, he sees a man at work, shovelling the accumulated snow, even as he shivers in the cold. The shoemaker invites him into his warm dwelling, and shares a meal with him.

Time passes. The shoemaker waits till midnight. He has not seen Jesus, and disappointed as well as exhausted, he prepares to go to bed. As is his custom, he opens the Bible to read a passage from it, and he finds these words: "Whatever you do unto the least of the little ones, you verily do unto Me."

The old shoemaker's heart lifts up with joy and love, for he realises that Christ did visit him – not once, but several times in the day – in the person of his needy brothers.

Not Suitable

President Mckinley of the United States of America had to make a choice between two men – one of them was to be posted as an ambassador to a foreign country. He made his decision, which was not influenced by the qualifications or the seniority of the two men, but by an incident that he witnessed years ago.

At that time, Mckinley had been a member of the House of Representatives. He had boarded a streetcar one night and taken a vacant seat at the back. Shortly afterwards, a washerwoman boarded the car, carrying a heavy basket. She walked the length of the car, looking for a seat and not finding one, stood at the front of the car, her heavy basket making it difficult for her to balance herself in the narrow aisle.

As Mckinley watched, the man sitting in the seat next to her, shifted the newspaper he was reading, so

40

that he could avoid seeing her. Mckinley walked up the aisle, took the woman's basket from her, and led her to his seat, which he offered her. As for the man who had avoided seeing her – he was the man whom the President rejected later, for the post of the diplomat.

The man did not realise that a little act of selfishness had deprived him of a post that would have been the crowning honour of his life!

A Photo Opportunity

There was a man who announced that he would be distributing tins of milk powder among slum-dwellers. The poor people – old men, women and children – were invited to come and stand in rows. The milk-powder tins were brought out, and the poor people waited eagerly to receive them – but the man would not begin the distribution. Fifteen minutes passed, half an hour passed; one hour passed. The slum-dwellers grew restless. "Why aren't we getting the milk powder as promised?" they wanted to know.

The answer they got made no sense to them: because the photographer had not arrived!

The 'generous donor' was anxious to have his photograph taken in the act of distributing the milk powder. Until the photographer arrived, he could not turn on his generosity.

God Is Watching You!

One way to be vigilant in all that we think and say and do, is to be aware that God is omnipresent and omniscient, and is aware of all that we do. I am reminded of a little boy who was visiting his grandmother. There was a large picture of Sri Vishnu on the wall of her living room. Underneath the picture was the caption: *God is Watching You.*

The little boy became strangely quiet and subdued on seeing the picture. Noticing his mood, his grandmother asked him what the matter was.

"I suppose I must be good and behave myself here," replied the little boy. "If God is watching me, He is sure to punish me if I'm naughty."

"Not at all!" laughed the grandmother. "God is watching you all the time because He loves you so much that He can't take His eyes off you!"

This is the spirit with which we must cultivate good thoughts and positive emotions. Here is one of the simple prayers I often offer:

Tiny is the house of my heart,
O Lord, widen it that it may receive Thee!
Broken is the house of my heart — renew it,
That it may be worthy of Thee!
Unclean is the house of my heart,
May it be washed whiter than snow!
My deepest longing will be fulfilled
When Thou wilt dwell in the house
Of my heart forever and forever more – and I
shall live and move
And do my daily work in Thy radiant presence, Lord!

Determination Conquers All

Gautama Buddha, the Enlightened One, attained his goal only through dedicated determination and unflinching perseverance. Several were the holy men he came into contact with; numerous were the paths he trod; severe were the austerities he practised. At the end of it all, he was reduced to an emaciated, weakened man, almost crippled by self-inflicted torture. And his goal – enlightenment – was still nowhere in sight!

Gautama turned away from extreme austerity and penance. He took a little nourishment to revive his failing strength and sat down under the Bodhi tree. He was determined that he would not leave it until he had attained enlightenment. His body could wither away, his skin might shrivel and fall, his bones might crumble to powder – but he would not give up until the desired goal was achieved.

How can success – even the greatest spiritual triumph – evade such dedication and determination?

No Job Is Menial

Dr. Charles Mayo is renowned as the Founder of the world famous Mayo Clinic. Dr. Charlie, as he was popularly known among his friends, was once playing host to an English friend at his home in Rochester. The Englishman, when he retired for the night, put his shoes outside his bedroom door, expecting a servant to shine them by the morning.

Dr. Charles Mayo noticed the shoes outside his guest's room. He picked them up and cleaned them himself!

When the friend opened his door next morning, he was very pleased to see his shoes shining like new. Little did he realise that it was his distinguished host who had done the 'menial' job that is normally left to the lowest servants.

Dr. Mayo was a man who knew what it was to serve humbly!

To be able to serve humbly, many of us may have to give up our self-assertive nature. We have developed our individual personalities and therefore many a time it becomes difficult for us to bend. We find it difficult to give up our pampered ego. We need to realise that no job is menial, no job is too low for us.

Not for Me!

The great American Confederate leader, Robert Lee, was once travelling in a train, accompanied by several of his officers and soldiers. At a small station en route, a poor woman boarded the train. She was lean and emaciated, her clothes were shabby. Not a single soldier offered his seat to the poor woman, as she looked in vain for a place to sit, in the crowded compartment.

As she approached Lee's seat, he did not lose a moment before he rose gallantly, and requested her to take his seat. No sooner was this done, than the officers vied with each other to offer their seat to the General.

"No gentlemen," said Lee firmly. "If you cannot give your seat to a poor woman, you cannot give it to me!"

Giving without Questions

A profound awareness of others' needs, a deep sensitivity for others' sufferings came to Sadhu Vaswani when he was just a child. Sometimes, as he sat down to his meals and heard the cry of a

passing beggar, he would take away his food to share it with the hungry one. From the early years of his life, he was filled with the spirit of compassion for all who were in suffering and pain.

Again and again, his mother found him awake in the middle of cold, wintry nights.

"What keeps you awake, my child?" she would ask him. "Is it the cold of the winter? Then let me wrap around you one more blanket or quilt."

He said to her, "Mother, the cold I feel cannot be overcome by a hundred blankets or quilts!"

"I do not understand you, my child," said the mother. "Speak to me in plain words, not riddles!"

He said, "Mother, I am thinking of hundreds of homeless ones who, in this severe cold, are lying on the roadside. Their cold seems to pierce my frame."

Throughout his life, Sadhu Vaswani had this sense of identification with the poor and destitute. In later years, once when he was ill, he was unable to take solid food. He felt that he would like to taste an orange. Several oranges were brought to him. As he looked at them, his thoughts moved out to the sick people who lay in the poor patients' wards of the Government Hospital. Without tasting a single orange himself, he sent them all to the poor patients. And he said, "I feel satisfied. I feel as though I have eaten all the oranges!"

Many said to him, "When you give to the poor, you do not discriminate, you do not make sure if the person to whom you give is deserving or otherwise."

Sadhu Vaswani said, "The Lord gives without hesitation to a undeserving person like me. Who am I to enquire into the deserts of others?"

On one occasion, Sadhu Vaswani said in good humour, "The man who gives only to those whom he considers deserving has reason to pray that the Lord, in judging him, will not follow his example."

It's All in the Mind

There was a boy who was born with a severe physical disability. One of his legs was so weak, that he had to have a brace on it. At first, he was not at all bothered by this handicap. But when he started going to school, he became dejected. He could not run; he could not climb trees; he could not play games like all the other boys.

Sensing his depression, his father decided to take the boy to a famous temple in a distant town. It was said that when people prayed at the temple, miracles happened to them. It was also said that the handicapped people who went there, could throw away their braces and crutches and walk freely. They were healed completely.

Father and son set out on a pilgrimage to the temple. They entered the shrine, and offered fervent prayers for the boy's leg to be healed. Suddenly, the boy sensed a wonderful feeling of warmth within his heart. He felt that he had been truly healed. He opened his eyes and rose to his feet. He glanced at his leg – but it was as withered as ever.

"It's no use being here," he said to his father. "Let us go. God has not heard our prayer."

As he neared the temple gates, he had a wonderful sensation. He felt as if a great hand passed over him, and he cried out, "Father, Father! You were right! I am healed! I am healed!"

Startled, the father looked at his leg – and saw no sign of healing. The brace was very much in place.

"Father, God has not taken away the brace on my leg," the son explained. "But He has taken away the brace on my mind! I no longer feel handicapped. I no longer feel an inferiority complex."

Look Within for Your Treasure!

There is an old Hebrew story about a poor Rabbi named Rabbi Eizik who lived in Krakow. One night he dreamed that an angel ordered him to look for a buried treasure under a bridge leading to the King's palace in Prague. This dream reappeared thrice – and after the third time, Rabbi Eizik set out for Prague, determined to find the treasure.

When he arrived there, he was dismayed to find the bridge guarded by soldiers day and night. There was no question of setting out to dig for the treasure – he would be arrested immediately.

He waited near the bridge, forlorn, walking up and down from sunrise to sunset. When night fell, the captain of the guards came to him and asked kindly, "What is bothering you my friend? Can I be of any help to you at all?"

Rabbi Eizik was so emboldened by the captain's kindness and courtesy, that he blurted out the story

of his dream, which had brought him all the way from Krakow to Prague.

The captain laughed aloud, but not unsympathetically. "So, my friend," he said, "to follow your dream, you have worn out all that shoe leather and come all the way to Prague. Why, if I had so much faith in my dreams, I would have gone to Krakow to look for the buried treasure under the kitchen stove of a Jew named Rabbi Eizik. Wouldn't I have been a fool?"

Rabbi Eizik thanked the man for his kindness and travelled back home. He started digging for the treasure under his kitchen stove – and sure enough, he found it lying there!

With the money, he built a house of worship, where he thanked the Lord every day for helping him to understand that his treasure was not out there in some distant place – but where he himself was.

Marcel Proust, the distinguished French writer, tells us: "The real voyage of discovery consists not in seeking new landscapes but in having new eyes." Many of us hunger for something far away and yet-to-be, while everything we need actually resides within us!

A Change of Attire

Once, Gandhiji and Kasturba were visiting a village. While Gandhiji was busy talking to the men, Ba went among the women and spoke to them of cleanliness and personal hygiene. "You must bathe every day," she told them earnestly, "and change into clean, washed clothes."

A poor woman took Ba into her hut and said to her, "Ba, the only clothes I have are these which I'm wearing now. How can I change clothes and wash them daily?"

Ba was profoundly moved by the woman's plight. She spoke of the incident to Gandhiji later that day. "What can we do for them?" she asked him in anguish.

During those days Gandhiji used to wear the traditional Indian clothes – *dhoti, kurta, angavastra* and turban. Forthwith he decided that he would wear only a loincloth from then on – for so many of his brothers and sisters had no clothes on their backs!

I Ask for Nothing More!

ong ago, there was a wise and compassionate ruler, who was the Shah of Persia. He loved his people dearly; he took a personal interest in their welfare and did everything he could to make their lives better.

It was his custom to go out among his people, in disguise, so that he could move about unnoticed and find out about their needs and problems, firsthand.

One day, he disguised himself as a poor villager and went to visit the public bath. People came here to relax in the comfort of a warm steam bath, after a hectic day's work. A furnace, located in the cellar of the building, heated the water for the steam bath. A man was posted there to keep the furnace going, and to maintain the comfort-level of the hot water.

The Shah made his way down to the cellar and met this man. He was a poor old man, who led a lonely life. For most of the day, he was confined to the dark cellar, and to the uncomfortable heat of the furnace. He was thrilled that the 'villager' had come down to the basement to visit him – for no one ever bothered to go down there! He carried a simple meal with him, which he shared with the Shah. He earnestly requested him to visit the cellar whenever he could.

For the next few weeks, the Shah visited him every day. Then, at long last, he revealed his identity to the man and asked him what he wanted. "Tell me what you need and I shall give it to you," he told the man.

The old man looked into his ruler's eyes and said, "Royal Sire! You left your grand palace with its comforts and luxuries, to sit with me in this hot and airless basement. You shared my humble food with me and showed me your genuine care and concern. On other people you may bestow rich gifts, but to me you have given the most priceless of all gifts – you have given 'yourself'. I ask for nothing more!"

The Secret of Charlie's Success

Norman Vincent Peale tells us a beautiful story, which shows that what one needs most to succeed in business is not just money and business acumen – but the ability to care for people.

There was a man called Charlie, a quiet man who ran a grocery store in a small town. His grocery was part of a chain store. Charlie was doing fairly well in life, when came a bolt from the blue. Suddenly, the company decided to close down their branch in Charlie's hometown. Charlie was troubled. He was not sure if he could run a store on his own, for he did not have much capital.

Now Charlie loved people; he loved talking to them, and being of help to them. He knew most of his customers personally, and that was his greatest asset. The people who came to his store, knew that he was interested in them as people. And so Charlie's business flourished. He survived competition from a supermarket chain. And when he finally died, his was one of the biggest funerals in town. It seemed as if everyone in town had turned up to pay tribute to a man who was not just a grocer – but one who genuinely cared for his fellow human beings.

Help Your Brother!

There is a moving story about Sadhu Sundar Singh, who was once travelling across the Himalayas with a companion. It was winter, and a severe blizzard was raging. The conditions were indeed very trying. As they trudged ahead, they saw a man lying still, by the narrow mountain path. To all appearances, he seemed to be frozen lifeless in the lonely terrain.

The Sadhu stopped to revive him and to offer whatever help he could. But his companion was adamant that they should move on. "It's no use wasting your time over him," he argued. "He is past reviving. If you stop to help him, you will be in trouble too, for it is suicidal to stop anywhere in this weather. We must move ahead so that we can reach the next village before it is dark."

But the Sadhu did not have the heart to leave the dying man to his fate. Resolutely, he began to rub and chafe the man's hands and feet, hoping to give some warmth to his cold limbs. His companion was so annoyed that he walked away from there, without even looking back.

Ten minutes of vigorous rubbing did nothing for the stranger. Finally, Sadhu Sundar Singh lifted the man on his back and began to trudge painfully through the falling snow.

Call it a miracle if you like, or call it good *karma* which fructifies instantly. The warmth of the exercise made the Sadhu's body temperature rise, and this gradually revived the stranger. The strain of carrying the man also helped the Sadhu to withstand the cold and the two mutually sustained each other.

When they had travelled a couple of miles, they saw another body lying by the wayside. It was the Sadhu's companion, who had refused to stop earlier. He was indeed frozen to death. Alone, he had not the warmth to fight the storm.

His Stores Are Never Empty!

Even as a small child, Sadhu Vaswani found that the world was sad, was smitten with suffering. He knew that on his own, he could do nothing. However, there was One for whom nothing was impossible. And he had access to this One through prayer. Whenever he found someone in suffering and pain, he would go and sit in a silent corner and pray for him.

One day, his mother, Varan Devi, spoke to him of a close relative who had lost his job. He had a wife and children to support, and no savings laid up. The family was passing through a difficult time. "If only he can get a job with a salary of twenty rupees per month," the mother said, "the family would be able to breathe again."

At night, when Sadhu Vaswani went up to the terrace, he closed his eyes and prayed devoutly to God, asking Him to help the afflicted family. "Lord, all he needs is a job with a salary of twenty rupees," he prayed. And he continued to do so for seven days.

On the seventh day, the mother came and announced that their relative had been given a job with a salary of exactly twenty rupees a month. "God has heard your prayers," said the mother to her son. "In future, if I need anything, I will come to you and not approach your father."

"No, Ma," said the child, "we both will approach God, who alone is the Source of all that man may need and whose stores are never empty."

Compassion in Action

The well-known social reformer Ishwar Chandra Vidyasagar was walking along the streets of Kolkata. As he was passing through a run-down locality, he heard the sound of weeping and wailing emanating from a small tenement. Gently, he knocked at the door of the house. An old man, whose eyes were red and tear-rimmed, opened it.

"Dear Sir, I heard your heart wrenching sobs as I passed by," said Vidyasagar. "Would you care to tell me what is troubling you?"

"Of what avail would it be to tell you of my misery?" replied the old man. "Everyone wants to know my problems – but no one is ready to help me!"

On Vidyasagar's insistence, the old man at last poured his anguish out in words. A few years earlier, he had borrowed some money from a man, by mortgaging his house. He had fallen on lean days, and his debts had mounted. Now his creditor had gone to court and soon his house (the only property left to the family by his father and grandfather) would be confiscated. He and his family would be homeless.

Vidyasagar listened to his story patiently, noting the names and dates and the details. "I shall do my best to help you," he promised.

When the old man turned up in court for his hearing the following week, he was dumbfounded to hear that his case had been settled and all his debts had been paid up fully. His benefactor was none other than Vidyasagar!

Let My Music Move Them!

It was a bitter, cold day in London. At the corner of a street, an old blind man sat on a low stool, playing his violin. The tin cup placed near the stool was practically empty. The blind man's fingers were blue with cold, but passers-by hardly paid any attention to his music. Their hands were in their pockets – but only to protect them from the cold, and not to bring out any money for the poor man.

A well-dressed man stopped at the corner. "No luck?" he asked. "No body wants to open their wallets for you? Well then, we will make them do it!"

Briskly, he took the cheap violin the blind man was playing, and began to play on it. The cheap violin seemed to come to life – beautiful, heavenly music flowed from it. People were mesmerised by the music, and soon a small crowd had gathered around the blind man. Everyone listened, spellbound.

When the music stopped, the gentleman passed round his own hat, and contributions poured in, notes and coins filling the hat in no time. The stranger deposited all the money in the tin cup, and returned the bow and violin to the blind man.

"O sir! How can I thank you enough?" exclaimed the blind man. "May I know your name?"

"They call me Paganini," said the stranger, shaking his hand warmly. One of the world's greatest musicians had not thought it beneath him to play at a street-corner to help a brother in need.

Life Is a Loan

Sadhu Vaswani was once asked, "What is your religion?" His reply was truly significant. He said, "I know of no religion higher than the religion of unity and love, service and sacrifice."

For him, indeed, to live was to serve, to live was to love, to live was to bear the burdens of others and to live was to share his all with all.

One evening, as we were taking a walk on the roadside with Sadhu Vaswani, we saw a poor man lying underneath a tree. His clothes were tattered and torn; his feet were covered with mud. Sadhu Vaswani stopped at the sight of this man. He asked for a bucket of water to be brought. And when it was brought, this prince among men – he had but to lift up a finger and hundreds of us would rush to find out what his wish was – with his own hands he cleansed the body of the poor beggar and passed on to him his own shirt to wear! The poor man pointed to the cap on Sadhu Vaswani's head, and without the least hesitation, the Master passed on the cap to him. On that occasion he spoke certain words, which I can never, ever forget. He said, "This shirt and this cap and everything that I have, is a loan given to me to be passed on to those whose need is greater than mine."

Mark the word *loan* – everything that we have is a loan given to us, to be passed on to those whose need is greater than ours. Nothing belongs to us; nothing has been given to us absolutely; everything has been given to us as a loan – our time and our talents, our knowledge, our experience, our wisdom, our prestige, our influence in society, our bank accounts, our property and possessions, our life itself is a loan. In these simple words of the Master, are enshrined the seeds of humanity, a new world order, a new civilisation of service and sacrifice.

The following *subhashita* (gem of speech) is attributed to Sage Ved Vyas:

All the wisdom that is taught through innumerable books may be summed up, thus: "To serve humanity is meritorious, and to harm anyone is sinful."

He Answered My Prayer!

A pious lady was talking to her nephew about the efficacy of prayer. Suddenly, the little boy asked, "If I ask God to help me find my marbles, will He answer my prayer?"

"But of course!" the lady assured him. "He always answers our prayers."

"May I kneel down and pray to God now?" the boy asked.

His aunt having given her consent, the little boy knelt by his chair, closed his eyes and prayed silently. Then he rose, and went about his work contentedly. Next day, the lady asked him if he had found his marbles. She hoped that his simple faith would not be tested adversely.

"No aunt, I haven't found them," the boy replied. "But God has made me not want to find them!"

God does not always answer our prayers in the way we wish or expect; but if we are sincere, He will take from us the desire for what is contrary to His Will!

Bad Luck, Good Luck

There is a Chinese story of an old farmer, who had a weak, ailing horse for ploughing his field. One day, the old horse ran away to the hills.

The farmer's neighbours pursed their lips and offered their sympathy to him. "Such rotten luck!" they remarked.

"Bad luck? Good luck? Who knows?" replied the farmer, philosophically.

A week later, the old horse returned, bringing with it a herd of wild horses from the hills. This time, the neighbours swarmed around the farmer to congratulate him on his good luck.

"Good luck? Bad luck? Who can tell?" was his reply.

Some time later, while trying to tame one of the wild horses, the farmer's only son fell off its back and broke his leg.

Everyone thought that this was bad luck indeed.

"Bad luck? Good luck? I don't know," said the farmer.

A few weeks later, the king's army marched into the village and conscripted every able-bodied young man living there. The farmer's son, who was laid up with a broken leg, was let off, for he would be of no use to them.

Now what could this be – good luck or bad luck? Who can tell?

77

Something that seems to be bad on the surface may actually be good in disguise. And something that seems to be attractive and 'lucky' may actually be harmful to our best interests. The wise ones leave it to God to decide what is best for them. They know that all things turn out good for those who love God and accept His Will unconditionally.

Helping a Friend

ooker T. Washington was a renowned black educator. Soon after he became President of the Tuskegee Institute in Alabama, he was taking a walk in an exclusive locality of the town, when a wealthy white woman stopped him.

"How would you like to earn a few dollars?" she asked him patronisingly. She did not know this famous man by sight. "I need some wood to be chopped."

Prof. Washington smiled, rolled up his sleeves and set to work. Soon the wood was chopped. He carried the logs into the house and neatly stacked them near the fireplace.

The woman's daughter recognised the famous scholar and was dumbfounded. When he had left, she gave her ignorant mother a piece of her mind.

Next morning, the contrite woman arrived at his office in the Institute and apologised profusely.

"It 's perfectly all right, Madam," replied Washington. "I enjoy a little manual labour occasionally. Besides, it is always a pleasure to do something for a friend!"

The lady was so impressed with this gracious attitude that she was instrumental in persuading several of her wealthy acquaintances to donate money for the Tuskegee Institute.

Rivals and Friends

Tony was an Italian. Ivan was a Russian. Both men had salon shops, which conducted brisk business. But the competition between them was healthy, and each one was good at his work.

One week, Tony found that there was a large increase in his clientele. He learnt that his competitor was ill, and had shut down his shop for one week. Tony worked late every day during that week and made a lot of money – over and above his usual intake. On Sunday, he put on his best suit. He took all the money he had made during the overtime hours that week, and put it in an envelope. He visited Ivan, who was convalescing at home. "There is a little present for you, Ivan," he said, handing over the envelope to his competitor. "Get well soon, I miss you!" With a bright smile and a warm handshake he was gone.

Fix Your Goal

When Abraham Lincoln was a young boy, he husked corn for three days so that he could earn a little money, to pay for a second-hand copy of *The Life of Washington*. He read the book avidly, and said to a woman he knew, Mrs. Crawford by name: "I don't always intend to do this you know – delve, grub, husk corn, split rails and the like."

"What do you want to be, then?" asked Mrs. Crawford.

"I shall be the President," announced Abraham Lincoln. "I shall study and get ready, and the chance will come."

The chance came and Abraham was ready to take on the most powerful position in the land – for he had fixed his goal early!

It has been said that winners make goals, while losers make excuses!

Life, Not Words

I recall having read many years ago, concerning an eminent Confucian scholar. He was 80 years of age, and it was believed that no one could equal him in China, in learning and understanding.

One day he learnt that far, far away a new doctrine had sprung up, that was profoundly deeper than his knowledge. This upset him. He lost his interest in life. He decided that the issue must be settled one way or the other.

He undertook a long journey, traversed many miles and met the master of the new Zen school. He asked him to explain the new doctrine. In answer, the Buddhist monk said to him: "Venerated Sir, the doctrine we propagate is a very simple one. It can be summed up in one sentence: 'To avoid doing evil, do as much good as possible'. This is the teaching of all the Buddhas."

On hearing this, the old Confucian scholar flared up and said: "What do you mean? I have come here facing the dangers and hazards of a long, perilous journey and in spite of my advanced age. And you just quote a little jingle that every three-year-old child knows by heart! Are you mocking at me?"

The Zen master very politely, answered: "I am not mocking at you. But please consider that though every three-year-old child knows these words by heart, yet even a man of eighty fails to live up to them!"

The Prayer of Surrender

There was a queen of a faraway realm, who was known for her piety and devotion. Her baby princess fell ill, and the best doctors in the kingdom were asked to attend on the child. However, despite the best medical help, the child steadily grew worse.

Day and night, the queen prayed fervently to God, even as she cared for her ailing child, and attended to her every cry and whisper. "Lord, help my child," she prayed. "May Your healing touch be upon her, and make her better!"

But the child did not get better. In fact, as days passed, her condition deteriorated until, finally, the doctors gave up all hope and told the queen that they could not do anything more for the child.

A holy man, who was visiting the palace at that time, suggested to the queen that she should try the most efficacious of all prayers – the prayer of surrender.

"What is the prayer of surrender?" asked the queen. "You surrender your child to God absolutely," explained the holy man. "It becomes His responsibility to do with the child as He wills. You do not have to ask anything on her behalf anymore."

The queen sank on her knees and prayed fervently, "O Lord, this child is no longer mine. She is Thine. I surrender her to Thee absolutely. Do with her as Thou will."

Tears flowed from her eyes even as she uttered the words – for what mother could say of her child, "This child is not mine, but Thine!" People can let go of many things – but not their own flesh and blood!

With great effort, the queen persisted with her prayer of surrender. Even as the child lay unconscious, she repeated, "This child is not mine, but Thine. I surrender her unto Thee. Do with her as Thou will."

Gradually, the child grew better. The doctors gasped at the miracle unfolding before their eyes as the child whom they had given up for lost, revived and returned in course of time to good health.

The prayer of surrender is perhaps the most difficult form of prayer. It puts our faith to the ultimate test – that of surrendering our hopes and fears, even our very will to live, to the Will of God. How many of us can say to Him in absolute surrender – "Not my will, but Thy Will, be done!"

It's Krishna!

There was a poor labourer, called Jagdish, for whom life was one long round of toil and sweat. He worked hard from dawn to dusk to feed his family – his very existence was a struggle.

Every morning on his way, he passed a temple. He could never have the luxury of stepping in for a moment of peace, for there was no time. But he had got into the habit of stopping at the gate of the temple, and closing his eyes in prayer for a brief moment.

He felt close to the Lord Sri Krishna in that moment! He saw the Lord before him, in his mind's eye, smiling at him; in his delight and pleasure at being so close to God, he would murmur softly, "Krishna, it's Jagdish!"

The same words were repeated when he returned from work, late at night. The temple would be in darkness; its gates locked up. But Jagdish would pause, close his eyes, shut out the world and greet God with those familiar, simple words: "Krishna, it's Jagdish!"

Years passed by. One day, Jagdish met with an accident at work. He had fractured his leg. His co-workers carried him home after a doctor had attended to him. He would be confined to bed for six weeks, he was told.

As darkness fell, Jagdish's heart instinctively thought of his evening tryst with the Lord. Today of course, it would not be possible. Here he lay, unable to move...

Jagdish closed his eyes, overcome by weariness and despair. A soft, sweet voice whispered: "Jagdish, it's Krishna!" The Lord had come to keep His appointment on time, when Jagdish was unable to do so!

God does not care for the form, the shape, the vocabulary of our prayer. It is the feeling that counts.

What's Inside Counts!

little girl found an abandoned kitten in her garden, and adopted the little creature as her pet. She looked after the kitten with great care, feeding it milk, and putting it in a cosy basket lined with old towels. The kitten grew up fast, and became her friend and playmate at home.

Tragically, it was killed in an accident few months later. The little girl was inconsolable!

Her grandmother, a wealthy lady, bought an expensive Persian cat and presented it to the girl.

"Thank you," said the little girl politely, with downcast eyes.

"Come on my dear," remonstrated the old lady. "Your Tommy was a stray cat, and I have replaced him with a fine and expensive kitten! You could surely show little more feelings for your new pet!"

The child swallowed a lump in her throat as she replied, "But grandma, you don't seem to understand! It's not the outside, but the inside of the kitten that counts!"

He Is There When You Need Him

The famous Scottish preacher, John McNeil, once related this moving personal incident from his life:

As a boy, little John went to work at a place far away from home. Every day he had to walk back home through a dense forest and across a lonely ravine. People said wild animals and notorious criminals roamed the ravine. Little John would cross the ravine every day in absolute dread. What if... what if...

One night, he was very late getting back from work. The moon was hidden behind dark, threatening clouds. The ravine was in pitch darkness as the little boy made his way across, his heart beating in cold terror. Footsteps seemed to follow him, and a voice was heard in the distance.

John McNeil stopped. He couldn't walk any further. He felt he could not even breathe. So terrified

was he! Now he heard the footfall clearly, and the voice called out, "John, John!"

It was his father's voice!

Knowing that the boy was late and being aware of his fear of the ravine, the father had decided to go out and meet his son, so that they could walk together across the ravine.

Out of the darkness, the loving figure of the father emerged, and took the boy by the hand. The boy felt the father's arms around him – and it was the sweetest and most wonderful sensation of his life!

"His coming changed the whole experience for me," John McNeil would recall, in later days.

God is your Father and my Father. In times of despair and darkness, we can hear His voice – for He will unfailingly come to meet us. He will be there, when we need Him. All we have to do is trust Him absolutely and completely.

A Beggar Becomes a Businessman

There is a beautiful story, told us, of a wealthy businessman in New York. As he was walking briskly to his office one morning, he came upon a destitute who had put out some dry, withered flowers for sale, and was holding out his cap to passers-by. The wealthy man tossed a dollar into the cap and hurried on his way. Suddenly, he stopped short and retraced his way to the beggar. "I'm sorry, friend," he said. "In my hurry, I forgot to pick up my purchase." He looked carefully at the withered flowers in the man's collection, and pulled out a dahlia. "My favourite flower," he smiled. "After all, you too are a businessman like me!"

A few months later, he was dining at a restaurant when a well-dressed, handsome man approached his table and introduced himself. "Perhaps you don't recognise me," he said. "But you are the man who helped me to make something of myself. I was just a vagabond selling flowers; you gave me back my self-respect. Now, I call myself a businessman, just as you did that day!"

It was not just charity that the wealthy man had given. He had given the poor man respect and dignity, which are far more valuable than money.

The Best News

Roberto de Vincenzo, the great Argentine golfer, had won a tournament. He received a cheque for the prize money, and was photographed by press representatives.

As he was about to drive away in his car, a woman in shabby clothes approached him.

"I congratulate you on your victory," she told him. "In your moment of triumph, I beg you to help a fellow human being in distress."

"Is there anything I can do for you?" asked the champion.

"My little daughter is seriously ill," said the young woman. "The doctors aren't giving me any hope, and I have so many bills pending, I don't know what to do!"

De Vincenzo was so touched by her story that he took out the cheque he had just received and endorsed it in the name of the woman. "I hope your child will be well soon," he said, as he handed the cheque over to her.

A few days later, he was lunching at the golf club when an official came up to him. "The parking attendants told me you were approached by a young woman last week," he said. "I wish to warn you, that woman is a fraud. She is not married. She has no sick baby. Don't let her cheat you."

"You mean there is no dying child?" said De Vincenzo.

"That's right," said the official.

"Thank God for that!" acclaimed the champion. "That's the best news I have had this week!"

He had offered his service without judgement – and that is the best kind of service.

Service – a *Sadhana*

everal years ago, a little girl was among a group
of spectators who stood before a beautiful
painting entitled "Christ before Pilate". It depicted
the moving scene of Pilate metaphorically washing
his hands off, before Christ was sentenced to
crucifixion. While everyone gazed at the picture with
awe, the little girl cried out impulsively, "Will no one
come to help Him?"

That little girl was Evangeline Booth, who went
on to become the Chief of the Salvation Army – a
worldwide humanitarian organisation, which has
indeed made service a spiritual discipline.

There is an amusing statement which says: "The
young people wish to change the world; the old
people wish to change the young." The men and
women of true service do not wish to change the
world or reform society with their service. Their only
aim is to make their service a spiritual *sadhana*, which

may bring about a change for the better within themselves – renew, reshape and reform the soul within. To such men and women, service is the way to God-realisation.

Never, Never, Never Give Up!

A distinguished scientist was supervising his students in the laboratory, when an experiment failed to produce the desired results. The students were disappointed, and their faces fell.

"Gentlemen," said the scientist, "when you are face to face with a difficulty, you are up against a discovery!"

Many are the discoveries, made by scientists who never, never, never gave up, when defeat stared at them.

Consider for a moment, the countless examples from history, of people who never, never, never gave up!

Henry Ford failed and went broke five times, before he finally attained success.

Beethoven was not defeated by deafness. He transcended his handicap to compose the most magnificent symphonies.

John Bunyan wrote *Pilgrim's Progress* while he was confined to a prison for his attempt to preach religion.

Deaf, speechless and blind since early childhood, Helen Keller achieved the kind of greatness that few people have ever achieved.

The difference between the impossible and the possible, it is said, lies in a man's determination. Never, never, never give up!

The Fire-Worshipper

An eastern legend tells us that Prophet Abraham was seated at his tent one evening, waiting to entertain strangers who were traversing the inhospitable desert. Soon he saw an old man walking towards him. He was weak and exhausted, leaning heavily on his staff, stooping as he walked.

The patriarch went out to greet him, leading him by the hand into his tent, where a warm meal was set before him.

The old man was so hungry that he partook the meal without saying a prayer.

"Of what faith are you friend?" enquired Abraham.

"Oh, I worship fire," said the stranger, as he ate. "I acknowledge no other God."

Abraham was so angered by this answer that he thrust the old man out of his tent, leaving him to fend for himself in the darkness of the night, exposed to the sky and the winds.

As Abraham retired to bed that night, God called to him and asked him where his guest was.

"I thrust him out, Lord," explained Abraham, "because he did not worship Thee."

God shook his head and said to him, "I have tolerated him all these years, although he did not honour me. Could you not tolerate him for one night, although he gave you no trouble?"

Hearing God's remonstrance, Abraham was ashamed of his intolerance. He went out in search of the weary stranger and invited him back to his tent, and offered him hospitable entertainment for the night.

I Have a Room for You!

read a beautiful story about an elementary school in Chicago, where the children got together to put up a Christmas pageant. A third grader was to play the role of the innkeeper. He had but one line of dialogue to deliver: "Sorry, there is no room at this inn."

However, the spirit of Christmas entered into this little boy, and he played his part with real feelings. "Sorry," he said to Mary and Joseph, "there is no room at this inn." But as they turned away, the little fellow called out, "Come back, Joseph, come back! I will give you my room!"

Perhaps, this is why Jesus told his disciples to become like little children!

The Widow's Mite

A special collection was being made for earthquake victims during a public discourse by a religious leader. As the collection box was brought to a wealthy man, he said to the volunteer, "Here's ten dollars. I thank God I can give it away and not feel it!"

The volunteer advised him gently, "In that case brother, make it twenty dollars, and *feel it!* The blessing really comes, when you feel it!"

Some folks give their mite,
Others give with their might,
And some don't give who might

What we give, we must give as an offering to God.

A wealthy man was approached by a charitable organisation for a donation. "I'll give my mite," said the prosperous merchant, as he drew out a single currency note from his wallet carefully.

107

"Do you mean the widow's mite, by any chance?" enquired the volunteer.

"Why, yes!" laughed the merchant. "It is not how much I give that matters. That is the widow's mite, isn't it?"

"I will be satisfied with half that much," replied the volunteer. "May I ask you how much you are worth?"

"Oh, about fifty lakhs," said the merchant.

"Then just give me twenty-five lakhs," said the volunteer. "That will be just half the widow's mite, for she gave *all* that she had!"

Charity with Courtesy

A little boy was walking down the Rue Royale in Paris with his grandfather, who was a kind and courteous gentleman. They passed by a blind man, who was seated on a low stool, begging for alms. The grandfather gave four coins to the boy and asked him to put them in the blind man's hat.

The boy dropped the coins into the hat and resumed his walk.

"You should have touched your hat before the gentleman," his grandfather suggested, mildly.

"Why should I do that?" asked the little boy.

"One should always do it when one is giving alms," the grandfather replied. "It shows your courtesy and good manners."

"But this man is blind," persisted the boy. "He can't even see me touch my hat for him."

"He may be a fraud," said the grandfather. The old man had no desire to reprove the man if he was pretending to be blind – but he had no wish to fail in his courtesy to a beggar.

Not for Fame or Money

Miners all over the world use Davy's Safety Lamp when they descend into the dark and deep mineshafts to carry out their work of digging for coal or other minerals. Dangerous inflammable gases are found in the depths of the earth, and there is constant danger of fire, which could prove fatal underground. Therefore, ordinary lamps cannot be used in the mines.

The man who invented the Safety Lamp was Sir Humphrey Davy. He had to work hard for several years, before his experiments led him to design the lamp, which would not set fire to the gases in the mineshaft. The Safety Lamp was, thus, a great boon and blessing to the miners.

Davy could have made a fortune out of his unique invention. But he did not do so. His valuable work was offered freely to the miners. When friends urged him not to lose the opportunity to make money out of his invention, Davy's reply was categorical. "It was not my intention to gain fame or make a fortune out of my work," he said. "I don't think these things can give me happiness. But I did want to help the men who work in the mines. My lamp will make life just a little easier for them, and this gives me the greatest satisfaction."

Little wonder then, that Sir Humphrey Davy is remembered today as a great scientist, and a benefactor of humanity!

Here's Something Better!

I always tell my friends that God answers our prayers in one of four ways.

In answer to some prayers, He tells us, "Yes! Here is what you wanted." This is the reply that most of us like to get. But it is not always given to us.

At times, God tells us, "No!" Though we may not like it at first, we will eventually realise that this negative answer was actually in our own interest.

At other times, He tells us, "Wait!" This means the time is not yet ripe for what we desire, and God in His wisdom, defers the answer.

In answer to some of our prayers, God says, "Here is something better!"

Columbus set out to find a shorter route to India. He prayed fervently for success in his venture. His prayers were answered with something better than

113

finding a shorter route to India; Columbus became the world-famous discoverer of America.

Pasteur, the great French scientist, prayed that he might find a cure for a disease rampant among cattle. He discovered something far more valuable to human beings – a cure for rabies, the dreaded dog-madness disease.

There was a tradesman who owned a little shop. His business would not pick up. He incurred many debts, and his creditors pursued him wherever he went. He was dejected and frustrated and decided to commit suicide.

He bought a vial of poison, and was about to take it to his lips when he heard a knock at the door. He put the poison aside and went to open the door, and found a postman waiting for him with a telegram. The telegram read, "Hearty congratulations! You have won the first prize in our lottery. A cheque for ten lakhs is on its way to you."

The man was about to swallow the poison, which would have ended his life. If the postman had knocked five minutes later, it would have been too late! We do not know what awaits us at the next turn.

But God knows, God sees, and He gives us what we *need* – though not always what we *want* – at the right time.

The Prayer of Affirmation

I read about a woman, who was haunted by a constant fear for the life of her children. Every time they went to school, she was desperate until they returned home. Every time they crossed the street, she held her breath in anxiety – even though there were so many people around them.

Someone said to her, "Why don't you practise the prayer of affirmation?"

"What is the prayer of affirmation?" asked the woman. "It means nothing to me."

The friend explained to her, what the prayer of affirmation was all about. Every time she became anxious about her children, she was told to repeat this prayer: "My Lord, God! My children are under your divine protection. I have no fear for them. I have cast out all fear, for I have surrendered my children into Your safe hands. Wherever they are, I know, You take care of them at every step, every round of life. Please accept my thanks for protecting my children." The woman conquered her irrational fear completely, through this prayer of affirmation.

And Sri Krishna Came ...

There was a young woman, who was a great devotee of Lord Krishna. She spent the better part of her day in prayer, *puja* and repetition of the Name Divine. Her one devout wish was to see the Lord in person, welcome Him into her home, and offer her devoted service at His Lotus Feet.

One night, Sri Krishna appeared in her dream. "I shall visit your home tomorrow," He said to her. "Please be on the lookout for me."

The girl's joy knew no bounds. She was up with the lark next morning. She washed and cleaned and polished, till every nook and corner of her home shone. With her own hands she prepared a delicious spread of eats, to offer to the Lord when He came. When everything was ready, she ran to the front door, and sat on the steps, looking for Sri Krishna's arrival.

An old man hobbled up, leaning on a stick. "Dear sister, you are the very picture of kindness," he said. "Would you be so good as to lead me to the nearest hospital? I need a pair of crutches, and the doctors may be able to help me."

"I would have gladly helped you, Baba," said the girl. "But not today, please! The Lord has promised to be here with me today, and I have no time for anyone but Him!"

Disappointed, the old man hobbled away. A little later, a *fakir* (mendicant) approached her door. He sang a beautiful song, and then requested her to give him some food — for he was hungry, and had a long way to travel.

"I would gladly give you food, brother," she said, "but not today, please! The Lord has promised that He will be with me today, and all the food in my home has to be offered to Him before I offer it to anyone else. I beg your pardon — but today, I have no time for anyone but Him!"

The *fakir* smiled at her, and went on his way.

The girl grew anxious as the hours passed. There was no sign of Sri Krishna!

A poor woman came along, with a baby in her arms and two little children following her. She said to the girl, "May the Lord bless you sister! Give us alms in His Name, for we are poor and needy. Give us something, in your charity and generosity, and be richly blessed by the Lord!"

"Yes, yes," said the girl hastily. "But not today, please! The Lord is visiting me, and I have time for no one but Him! Please go away now; if you come tomorrow, I will give you everything that you need."

The woman begged and pleaded – but to no avail. She too, moved on, disappointed.

Darkness fell. The girl sat on the steps, still waiting. The moon and stars appeared. Gradually, the world went to sleep and all was silent. The girl rose from the steps. Her eyes were filled with tears. She went before the *murthi* of Sri Krishna, which she worshipped and fell at His Feet. As she had kept awake throughout the day with unblinking eyes waiting for the Lord to appear before her, her eyes were tired and she dropped off to sleep.

She had a dream. In the dream Sri Krishna appeared before her. Immediately, she cried: "How could You do this to me, Lord? You promised me You would come — and You have not kept Your word!"

"I kept my word to you!" she heard the Lord say. "I came to you for help and assistance. I came to you not once, but thrice – but you turned Me away!"

The Lord's Way

Two boys in a Boarding School were assigned rather menial tasks involving manual labour — such as cleaning tables after meals, mopping floors and so on. One of the boys was very unhappy with this kind of work. He rushed through the jobs hastily, unsatisfactorily, and would skip off to play.

The other boy, observing this, would not only do his allotted task well, but also do his best to complete the other boy's work.

The teacher in charge noticed this, and he asked the diligent boy what prompted him to do another's work. The boy's reply was significant. "The Lord tells us — *Whosoever will be great among you, let him be a servant of all*. It is this kind of greatness I aspire to and so I am trying the Lord's way!"

A Gift to God

A poor but devout woman wanted to give away some of her old clothes to earthquake victims in Gujarat. "I can give away some of my blankets and bed sheets," she thought. "They need it more than I do – for they are without homes, and camping out in the open air." But she did not bundle up her old sheets and pass them on to the collector. Instead, she carefully washed them, dried them, mended them and then handed them over to the collector. "This is meant for God's children," she said. "And so I wanted to make it as nice as possible."

Is it not true that we are rather careless when we give away old clothes for the poor and the needy? Do we not dump the unwanted, the unusable and the useless as 'offerings' to the collectors? And yet, we take such care to choose gifts and wrap them up carefully for our friends, our near and dear ones. Our offerings to the needy too, must be treated as gifts – to God.

A Humble Request

St. Augustine of Hippo strongly disliked loose talk and gossip. He had the following verses put up on the wall of the room where guests were usually entertained.

> Slanderer, beware!
> This is no place for thee.
> Here, naught shall reign
> But truth and charity.

Very often, his guests ignored the warning lines, and would indulge in uncharitable talk. On such occasions, the saint did not reproach them or upbraid them.

"My friends," he would tell them kindly but gravely, "you must either stop talking in this manner, or it will be necessary for me to blot out these lines."

People who heard this gentle request never again dared to indulge in unkind talk!

Slow and Steady

Charles Swindoll once found himself having to deal with several pressing commitments within a short span of time. He became tense and panic-stricken. He was snapping at his wife; gobbling his food at mealtime.

"These were classic symptoms of irritation," he recalled. "Before long, it all began to recoil upon me. The peace of my home was lost completely."

One evening at dinner, he found that his little daughter was trying to tell him something. Earnest and anxious, she came up to him and said, "Papa! Something exciting happened at school today. Can I say it to you very quickly?"

Something awoke in Swindoll. He hugged his little girl and said to her, "Tell me everything, honey! And you don't have to hurry. Tell me *slowly*."

"I'll tell you slowly, Papa," said the child. "But are you sure you can *listen* slowly?"

How much do we lose out on the little joys of life when we cannot walk, talk, think or *listen* slowly!

Get Connected to God!

A man went to his Guru, complaining of utter fatigue and exhaustion. "Swamiji, I just cannot cope any more," he complained. "Please help me!"

The Guru took him to an inner chamber, where there were two clocks on the table. Both were ticking away merrily. One was a clock that needed to be wound every day; the other was connected to the mains with a power cable.

"This clock will keep ticking for no more than 24 hours," said the Guru, pointing to the first one. "After just one day, it will slow down and begin to lose time gradually. I have to come in every morning and wind it up, to keep it going, or else it will soon come to a stop."

He pointed to the electric clock. "This one you can see, is connected to a source of high power, and with the energy from that source, it keeps going, on and on. It does not need to be wound up every day. It just goes on, ticking merrily."

The man stared at the two clocks, unable to understand what the Guru was saying.

"You must connect yourself to God – the Source of the highest, purest and best energy in the Universe," said the Guru. "Then you will not have to be pushed from outside. No one will have to wind you, or give you a boost. You will draw all the energy and wisdom of the Universe through your connection with God, and nothing can stop you!"

The world looks bleak and miserable to those who are fatigued. Give the body enough sleep; recharge your heart and soul by connecting yourself to God constantly. Then, your soul can work to relieve your stress and restore your depleted energy.

The Tenfold Gift

Two wealthy sheikhs once visited Rabia, the revered woman-saint of Islam. They had travelled very far in their piety and devotion, and were quite hungry when they arrived. However, they were confident that the saint would offer them food that could be accepted under Islamic law.

Having greeted them and welcomed them to her humble abode, Rabia set before them two hard loaves of bread. But at that very moment, a beggar arrived at Rabia's door, asking for alms. Without a moment's hesitation Rabia took away both the loaves and gave them to the beggar.

Her guests were astounded by her behaviour. The hard loaves would have been as welcome to them as any royal banquet – so hungry were they! But their respect for the saint was so high that they did not complain.

Just then, a maidservant entered Rabia's cottage with a covered tray. The smell of freshly baked bread filled the cottage as she placed the tray before Rabia and uncovered it. On it were 18 loaves, still warm from the oven.

"My mistress sent these for you," the maid said to Rabia. The eyes of the guests widened in amazement. Here was a saint indeed! Why, this was nothing short of a miracle! They would now be offered the soft, fresh loaves, which had arrived as if she had ordered them for the guests specially!

As they looked on, Rabia glanced at the loaves for a while. Then she said, "I'm afraid there must be some mistake. Please take them back to your mistress."

The maid was taken aback and tried to protest. But Rabia insisted that the loaves be taken back, and so it was done.

When the maid took the loaves back to her mistress, she was asked to recount the story as it happened. The mistress heard her out, and then added two more loaves to the tray. "Now, take these back to the saint," she told the girl.

Once more, the tray was set before Rabia. The saint graciously acknowledged the gift of twenty loaves and blessed the maid and her mistress. Then she laid the freshly baked loaves before her guests and requested them to eat. "You must be very hungry," she said to them with a smile.

Surprised by the turn of events, the two men ate heartily. After the meal, they ventured to ask Rabia, "O saint of God, please explain to us the mystery and significance of the events we have just witnessed."

"When you both arrived," Rabia explained, "I saw that you were hungry and tired. All I had were two cold loaves, and I felt it would be too meagre a fare to set before you. Therefore, when the beggar came, I bestowed the two loaves on him, and said to the Lord, O God, you have promised that that you will repay our charity tenfold. This is beyond doubt. I offer these two loaves to the beggar in your name: grant me a tenfold return on them so that I may feed my hungry guests!'

"You saw that the maid servant brought me a gift of loaves from her mistress. When I saw that there were only 18, I realised that there was a mistake and so I sent her back. When the right amount that I had petitioned for arrived, I accepted the gift gratefully.

"You see, God always keeps His word to us!"

Gandhi and Tagore

We are accustomed to think of great men as if they were solemn, pompous, monumental figures living on an elevated intellectual plane way above the rest of us. How wonderful it is to realise that they were human beings, blessed with a delightful sense of humour!

When Gandhiji visited Shanti Niketan, he was respectfully escorted to a beautifully decorated chamber, which was to be his lodging during the whole duration of his stay.

Gandhiji, who was given to a life of utter simplicity, turned to Tagore and remarked, "Why have you brought me to this bridal chamber?" With a twinkle in his eye, he added, "And where is the bride, if one may ask?"

"Shanti Niketan, the ever young queen of our hearts, is here to welcome you," replied Tagore, rising to the occasion.

"But surely, the queen of your hearts would hardly care to look twice at an old, toothless pauper like myself," laughed Gandhiji.

"On the other hand," retorted Tagore, "our queen has always loved Truth and worshipped it all these years."

"Ah, then there is hope even for old, toothless paupers," laughed Gandhiji.

The bridal chamber echoed the hearty laughter of everyone present!

Book of Noble Conduct

St. Serapio of Egypt was one who bore witness to the great precept of the religion of service in deeds of daily living. His most valuable raiment was a long coat of very coarse cloth, which he often pawned, and once sold outright to help the poor and needy. At times, he would even pawn himself – commit himself to prolonged manual labour for a certain period of time, working for a rich man – so that he could obtain money to feed the poor.

One of his close friends was shocked to see him in tattered clothes, on one occasion. "What is the matter?" he remonstrated. "Why are you so famished and unclothed?"

"The answer to that question is to be realised – not interrogated," was the saint's reply. "I cannot bear to see helpless ones suffer. My *Book of Noble Conduct* tells me that I must sell off all my belongings to serve the poor and the needy."

"May I see this *Book of Noble Conduct* which you regard so highly?" enquired the friend.

"That book has also been sold off to help my needy friends," the saint replied briskly. "It was sold for a noble purpose – and it will pay doubly, because the person who obtains it will be transformed by the spirit of service, and do all he can to help the desolate and destitute."

Such is the spirit of sincere service!

One Thing at a Time

They asked a woman-saint, "How did you arrive at the lofty heights you have reached? What was the *tapasya* you performed to attain such a state? We always find you smiling and cheerful. Pray, tell us what is the secret of this happy state!"

The saint replied, "My secret is a very simple one. When I eat, I eat. When I work, I work. When I sleep, I sleep."

The people were puzzled. They said to her, "But that is what we do, too! We eat when we eat; we work when we work and we sleep when we sleep." "No," she said. "When you eat, your mind travels far. You think of so many things that you are not even aware of the food you are eating. You don't enjoy the food. You should taste every morsel, chew it, swallow it. Alas, you don't do this! And when you work, you are thinking of a thousand things. You must live in the present!"

Let us learn to do only one thing at a time. Doing more than one thing divides your attention and multiplies your stress. When you are talking to someone, give him or her, your full attention. It may be just a little matter – but it saves you from considerable stress. Give your best to what you are doing at any given moment. Let all your energy and attention be focused on the task at hand. When the mind is one-pointed, it becomes capable of concentration and is free from tension.

Forgiveness, the Best Lubricant

A learned Professor of repute engaged a class at the University. Having delivered an introduction to his topic, he pointed to one of the students and asked him to read aloud from the text.

The student arose and began to read, holding his book in his left hand. "That's not the way to behave in class," said the Professor sharply. "Take your book in your right hand and be seated."

The student stopped short. After a moment or two, he silently held up his right arm – he did not have a right hand!

The class grew strangely silent. Everyone felt uncomfortable and pained.

The Professor sat still, dumbfounded. Then he rose from his seat and walked slowly down to where the young man stood. He put his arm around him and said with tears in his eyes, "I am truly sorry. I have spoken in haste. Will you please forgive me?"

Forgiveness is the precious lubricant which keeps all our relationships smooth and friction-free.

Let Us Thank the Lord

A group of pilgrims were on their way to a remote shrine in the mountains. The journey was a long and hazardous one. The narrow path was steep and slippery, and progress was slow. The weather was freezing, and food and water had to be carefully rationed. As the days passed, a feeling of gloom and pessimism descended over the group.

It was decided that, at the next night's stop, a meeting would be held to discuss their problems.

When the pilgrims gathered around the campfire that night, one of them began to speak. "Before we speak of anything else, let us thank the Lord for His grace and kindness. We have come thus far with no loss of life, and all of us are still on our feet."

Absolute silence followed the simple words of gratitude. No one had any complaints to make. Everyone felt that they were really fortunate to have come thus far.

Such is the change, the transformation that gratitude can bring about! A thankful heart enables us to look at the brighter side of life, and get the right perspective.

Painting Feet on a Snake

A Tao story tells us of an artist who was so gifted that his fame spread all over the land. One day, he painted the picture of a snake. It was so lifelike, so real that viewers seemed to hear it hiss!

They praised the picture to the skies. The artist was so carried away by his own success and the adulation of his fans that he started painting the picture again. He touched up the snake; he made its eyes glow; he outlined the fangs so that they seemed to dart at you! He could not stop; he went on and painted feet on the snake!

The expression, "Painting feet on a snake," has become a Chinese saying – an aphorism. It refers to situations that are needlessly made more complicated by people who do not know when and where to stop.

When our life becomes complicated with power and possessions, we move farther and farther away from the simple joys and pleasures of life. We fail to notice the green grass and the fresh morning flowers. We don't have time to hear birds sing or watch our little ones smile. We drift away from the state of childlike innocence and simple joy, which is our basic nature.

Just Laugh It Off!

There was a little girl who could not pronounce the word "Spaghetti". The more she tried, the funnier became her pronunciation.

"P-ppassghetti..." she would stammer. "Saphetti..." and she would end up in tears every time.

Her father advised her, "Don't take it so seriously, honey! If you can't pronounce a word – so what? Just laugh it off!"

This proved to be an excellent therapy. Next time she could not say "Spaghetti", she laughed out aloud. She was amazed when the others around her began to laugh with her. They were not laughing at her – in fact, everyone was having such fun!

As the girl grew older, she learnt to pronounce "Spaghetti" correctly. But every time she uttered the word right, she would think of the great fun she had with "Pasghetti" and "Gaspetti"!

People today, have forgotten to laugh. They have stopped smiling. What a sad loss this is!

Abu Othman and His Host

bu Othman al-Hiri was invited to a feast. When he arrived at the door of the house, his host appeared and said to him, "Sir, I cannot ask you to come in! So please go away – and may Allah have mercy upon you."

Abu Othman returned home wordlessly.

No sooner had he gone home, than the friend followed him inside, urging him to join the feast.
Abu Othman went with him. But when they got to the door of the house, the friend begged to be excused. He could not invite the holy man inside.

Without a murmur, Abu Othman turned to go. Once again, his host followed him, and the same pattern was repeated.

Now, Abu Othman was known to be a man of patience and even temper. He put up with this same treatment four times. At the end of it, the host fell at his feet and said, "Forgive me, Abu Othman. I have acted, thus, to put your temper to the test. Allow me to tell you how I admire your patience!"

"Praise me not," said Abu Othman, "for dogs can practise the same virtue; they come when they are called and retire when we chase them away."

There spoke a man of true humility!

Write It on Sand!

wo merchants were travelling along an inhospitable mountain-route which winds across the lonely, windswept hills of Persia. They were glad to have each other's company, for they were old friends. Each was accompanied by a retinue of servants and a caravan, which was carrying their merchandise.

As they were crossing a treacherous and narrow pass, one of them, a man called Najib, lost his footing and fell into a wild foaming river. The other merchant, known as Mussa, leaped in after him without hesitation and saved his friend from drowning.

The friends embraced each other with tears in their eyes. Then Najib called his most skilled slaves and ordered them to carve the following words on a huge black boulder that stood nearby:

"Wanderers! Know ye, that here in this wild and lonely spot, Mussa heroically saved the life of his friend, Najib."

The friends then continued on their journey.

Several years passed, and they happened to travel on the same route again. Reaching that very spot where one had saved the other's life, they got down to look around and relive an unforgettable memory.

They sat for a while, talking of this and that. Suddenly, they found themselves arguing about some trifling matter. A heated quarrel ensued. In a fit of anger, Mussa struck Najib on the face, and he fell down – on the very spot where they had embraced each other tearfully years ago.

Najib got up and looked at his friend for a minute. He then picked up a twig that lay nearby and wrote the following words on the white sand, near the huge black boulder:

"Wanderers! Know ye, that in this wild and lonely place, Mussa, after a trivial argument, broke the heart of his friend, Najib!"

One of Najib's slaves asked him, "Sire, you recorded your friend's heroism on the stone. Why is it that you write of his cruelty on the sand?"

Najib replied, "I shall cherish the memory of my friend's kindness and brave assistance in my heart forever. But the injury he inflicted on me, I hope, will fade away from my memory, even before these words fade from the sand!"

Forgive your friends – even before forgiveness is asked. And when you forgive – make sure you forget!

O, Let Them Live!

A little boy came into the house carrying a tiny black puppy. It looked ill – pathetically ill! It was just a bag of skin and bones!

The boy's mother set aside her housework to look at the little puppy that her son held out to show her. She shook her head in despair.

"Albert, Albert," she sighed. "You can't bring every stray animal and hurt bird into the house!" "But mother, if I didn't bring it in, what would happen to it?"

Two weeks earlier, he had brought in a wounded owl. Now it was a starving puppy. He lifted its head, so that its swollen, red, half-shut eyes could be plainly seen.

"That puppy is very sick, Albert," said the mother. "You can't keep it here."

"I know it's very sick, mother," Albert cut in quickly. "What will happen to it if I left it? Let me care for it, please! I promise you I will not trouble you or father."

A fortnight later, Albert brought the puppy in, to show his mother. It was round and plump. Its eyes were bright and clean, and its short tail was wagging away happily. "May I keep him?" pleaded Albert.

"Of course, you may," said the mother, without even thinking. Albert had taken full responsibility, as he always had!

Albert Schweitzer became a great physician and missionary in Africa. But he continued to help all living beings in God's creation, especially birds and animals. He nursed sick jungle animals, and stray dogs, cats and goats that wandered into his camp.

He was indeed, an embodiment of the spirit of compassion.

The Secret of Yoga

Bhartari, the leader of a group of *yogis*, met Guru Nanak. Bhartari was anxious to convert Guru Nanak to his cult.

"You don't have to wander from place to place," he said to Nanak, who was still a young man at the time. "Enter our fold! Permit me to put ear-rings in your ears and clothe you in the garments of a *yogi*! Let me make you a *siddha* and teach you how to live forever!"

Guru Nanak was greatly amused. He asked the venerable yogi, "Is it necessary to pierce one's ears in order to become a *yogi?* Yoga is the union of the individual with the Divine Spirit – it is not a matter of wearing certain ornaments or garments!"

The Guru added, "Outward forms and physical exercises are of no avail as long as the ego rules. If a man is to teach others, he must annihilate the ego

154

and make his mind pure – free from pride and attachment and anger."

Bhartari was annoyed. How could a young man like Nanak dare to question him? "Listen to me," he said harshly. "I inherit the wisdom of the centuries. Our system has endured from the beginning of time and its truth has never been challenged!"

Humbly answered the Guru, "I beg you not to be annoyed. Age is no evidence of the intrinsic merit of a system. Is it not true that good and evil have existed, side by side, from the beginning of time? The evidence of yoga is not age, but the elimination of the ego. The *yogi* is one who is singularly free from the evils of passions and pride, of greed and attachment and anger."

The Guru was indeed a true *yogi!*

Finding God

Rabia once sent three things to Hassan – a candle, a needle and a single strand of hair.

Asked to explain their significance, Rabia said: "Be like the candle which gives light to others and is itself consumed. And be like the needle which clothes others while it remains unclothed. When you live thus, a thousand years will be to you as a strand of hair!"

"Would you wish to marry me?" Hassan asked Rabia once.

Rabia answered, "Marriage is for those who have being. Here, being has disappeared, for I have become naught to the self and exist only through Him. I belong wholly to Him and do as He bids me to do. You must ask my hand of Him, not of me."

"Tell me Rabia," said Hassan, "how did you find this secret?"

Rabia answered, "I lost all things when I found Him."

My *All* for the Guru

Sant Eknath was a disciple of Janardhan Swami. The Swami was then a Governor in charge of a fort. Once a week, Janardhan Swami devoted a whole day to silence, meditation and communion with the Divine. Taking advantage of this, a Muslim king decided to attack the fort and capture it on the day of Janardhan's weekly retreat. He was sure that he could conquer the fort with ease, while the Governor sat in prayer and meditation.

At that time, Sant Eknath was a young boy of just sixteen or seventeen years. He heard of the enemy's onslaught, but was unafraid. He knew that it was his responsibility to defend the fort, while his Guru was in *dhyana*. The young man entered the Guru's room, put on the Guru's armour and took up the Guru's sword. He mounted his Guru's horse and led the Guru's army forward. He won the battle, routed the enemy, sent him fleeing and returned to the fort, victorious.

Quietly, he stabled the horse, returned the armour and the sword to the Guru's room, and attended the evening *satsang* in the Guru's presence, without uttering a word about his own fearless feat! Such was his spiritual strength, that he had been able to take on the burden of his Guru at a young age!

The Devoted Servant

The King of Ratnapuri was dying. He had no children and therefore, no successor to his throne. His Chancellor, a wise and a learned man, advised the King to choose his successor from among his most faithful followers.

The King summoned Sher Singh and Ramdas – his two devoted knights. Addressing the former first, he said, "Tell me Sher Singh, if I nominated you as my successor, how would you rule the people?"

"Your Majesty, I shall uphold the power and glory of the sovereign. I shall rule the people with an iron hand, and the laws will be imposed with due severity," said Sher Singh.

Turning to Ramdas, the King said, "What about you, Ramdas? What kind of king will you be?"

"I shall be a servant of all, your Majesty," Ramdas replied. "A true king is one who serves his people.

The only difference between him and other servants is that he sits on a throne. And so I shall continue to be to the people what I am to you – a devoted servant."

Ramdas was chosen to be the King's successor. One recalls the words of Sadhu Vaswani: "He is truly great – who greatly serves."

No Room for Fear

Hari was the guard and keeper of a hunting lodge located at the edge of a dense forest. There were rarely any visitors to the lonely place, but it was the royal decree that the house should always be well guarded and well maintained for the king and his courtiers who often went to hunt in the forest, and would use the lodge for a brief rest or even a night's stay.

One day, Hari received a royal decree from the palace. The king would stop by the following day for a meal and a nap. He was to get the best bedchamber ready and prepare a meal fit for the royal visitor.

Hari awoke early the next morning and carried out all the preparations systematically. The king's bedchamber was well aired and laid with the best linen. A piping hot meal was prepared and kept ready for the King.

Hours passed, and by 2 o'clock in the afternoon the King had not arrived. Hari stood near the gates of the lodge anxiously, awaiting the arrival of his Royal Master.

At about 3 o'clock, a battered, blood-strained and badly injured stranger tottered towards the gates of the lodge. Hari rushed out to hold him before he fell. The man had been mauled by a tiger. "Help me!" he cried to Hari. "Save me! I am dying!"

Hari led the stranger into the lodge. Hot water was kept ready for the King's bath. Hari used it to bathe and clean the stranger's wounds. He clothed the wounded man in the soft robes that had been laid out for the King. He coaxed the stranger to eat some food, feeding him with the choicest delicacies that had been prepared for the King. When the man had been fed, Hari led him to the King's bedchamber and put the exhausted man to sleep.

Shortly thereafter, the Diwan arrived at the lodge. He had come to inspect the preparations for the King's visit, and was incensed to hear Hari's account of the stranger. "You will answer for this gross misconduct!" he thundered. "How dare you offer the

King's hospitality to a passing beggar? How could you offer him food and drink before His Majesty had eaten? Who do you think is paying your salary? The King shall hear of this and you will be suitably punished..."

"The King has heard of his conduct already," said the voice from the bedchamber. The Diwan rushed into the room, and fell on his knees at the sight of the stranger. "Your Majesty," he gasped in amazement, "how is it that you are here all alone – and in this terrible condition?"

The King explained that his hunting party had been attacked by a band of fierce tigers. Some of his men had been killed and others badly wounded. A few had simply taken to their heels, leaving the injured King to fend for himself. He had half-crawled, half-walked his way to the lodge, where the kind-hearted

keeper had taken such good care of him. Awakened by the Diwan's angry outburst he had called out to tell him what had transpired. "I fell off my horse; I lost my weapons and I appeared before him like a wounded beggar," said the King. "He treated me with all the love and compassion that one human being can give to another. He fed me and served me like a King. He was not afraid of punishment or recrimination. He put service before self. He deserves the greatest reward that I can give!"

Love and compassion leave no room for fear!